Answer
To
Sentencing

Help Judges Cut Minimums

Reverend Mike Wanner

Table Of Contents

Introduction

Some sources report that in America alone that there are more than 2.3 million people in jail.

I like most people was entirely oblivious to that fact. I started channeling Angel Raphael in 2013 and began releasing little message sets as they came through.

In message set 16 of the Angel Raphael Speaks Series there was a message

"I asked Mike to Step into Prison Energetically

I have asked Mike to get the address and location within a prison of a designated space so he can visit energetically and receive feedback for us. Whether he will have time, interest or opportunity to do this will be interesting to see. As he writes this, he is not thrilled with the idea. We are already consuming a lot of his time."   ARS16

I had resisted that invitation to visit jail energetically until 2016.

1 - Why I am Writing This Book

The invitation that I referenced just above was finally embraced in 2016. So far, The Angel Raphael prodding has had me publish over fifty books about prison possibilities.

I focus on possibilities because the existing circumstances we find ourselves in is a progressive mess that is **NOT blamable** on any living being, so fault finding is a waste of time.

The old-time rule writers are all gone and so should be some of their protocols. Policies that are not relevant should go to the history books and not be referenced to new rulings.

2 - Disclaimer

I, the author, am not involved with prisons or prisoners but I have talked to many prisoners during Hospital Pastoral Visitations. I am sharing what is coming to me in an effort to spread understanding and trigger conversation that can be helpful. It may be that the discussion needs finessing and I invite your wisdom into the mix.

My guidance has suggested that a lot can be done. I will detail my views which are not the expert positions of a Corrections Officer or Corrections Administrator or Corrections Manager or Corrections Supervisor, or Medical Practitioner or Psychologist or Psychiatrist or Social Worker or another expert who might be helpful here.

As I have said many times before, everything that I look at about prisons seems to be so complicated. Here I reference my earlier book that suggested some things that have come to my awareness regarding United States Sentencing Commission 2010 Judges Survey that align with channeled messages from Angel Raphael.

Note

I have written five books titled Prison Possibilities Dialogue Series, and I invite submissions in the format specified. The core message about the series can be found for free at http://angelraphaelspeaks.com/prison-possible/

I also invite your consideration of the matter herein and opinions to further dialogue and progress.

3 - Why Would A Federal Judge Quit

There was a report in the news about a Federal Judge in Nashville who left the bench because he was uncomfortable living up to the duty of silence that comes with the robe. This got my attention because you do not hear about something like that very often.

It seems that mandatory minimum sentences had an impact on a case before the judge. The law required that the defendant is sentenced to life imprisonment.

Taking the robe off and resigning removed the duty to be quiet. The ex-judge could then go public with a declaration of his dissatisfaction with his commitment to sentencing the prisoner to life.

The judge denounced mandatory minimum sentences. Of course, the statement did not change the judgment that had been made that the prisoner is probably still serving now.

The Judge Is Not Alone

The story got my attention, so I did some googling and was very surprised at what I found. In my earlier book, I referenced elements that I found interesting.

About 50% of the judges in the survey said that some mandatory minimum sentences should be delinked, that seemed like a strong indication to me that we have work to do.

4 - Some Problems with Sentencing

The job of a Judge is not easy and the way I understand the story is that the sentence was mandatory for a person convicted of that particular crime. The Judge's outrage may or may not have been isolated to this specific case or merely the straw that broke the proverbial camel's back.

It seems that Prisons are often in the news, but there are few stories found about the successful rehabilitation of those within the walls.

In business, success is indicated by units of work or product created within that industry. If rehabilitations accomplished are the measurements of success for resources expensed within the prison industry, it may be that productivity is very low.

There is also the issue of protection for the community in that those in prison are not out on the streets posing a threat to the society. The protection factor is temporary in that almost all prisoners re-enter the neighborhood sometime.

In business, the absence of success usually involves the need for a reorganization of practices to do more of what helps and less of what does not. It could be that some restructuring might help those who manage prisons.

The ideas of reorganization are straightforward, but the business techniques may not easily compare to managing the human dynamics of prison.

It has been evident to me as I write my books that there is a great need for human resources expertize but it seems little budget ability to invest in the credentialed staff who can make the needed changes happen.

So like in many families when the budget is insufficient, the managers endeavor to do the best they can with the resources that are available. The difference between families and prisons is the investment of the participants.

Family members are influenced by their human plusses and minuses of their connectivity with all the others. Prison staff are less emotionally involved and have less authority and influence to create change.

Conflicts within families are usually short-lived and resolve without long-term consequences. Disputes within prisons can be must longer-lasting, and the results can be deadly.

One thing that could make a difference is the efficiency of using resources optimally and an excellent tool for doing that is controlling occupancy. Overcrowding is standard in many facilities, and that can be problematic.

We as a society have to get more realistic in developing resources that can improve the circumstances for prisoners. Prior to this book, I have written over fifty books about possibilities.

I offer my books for free on Kindle as often as I can according to the Kindle rules, and I invite you to the project.

You can embrace some new possibilities through the books by visiting the website http://angelraphaelspeaks.com/christmas/ And downloading them when they are free and then reading them when you are ready.

Free Kindle Books about Prison Possibilities rotate there and can be downloaded to your Kindle or a free Kindle app on any computer or phone. Before downloading, please confirm the price is showing at $0.00.

5 - Sentencing Sets the Stage

Mandatory minimum sentences set the stage for the mental devastation that deflates optimism, stagnates hope and programs unhappiness. Changing the sentencing criteria by the judges understanding can bring meaning that provides a more fertile field for collapsing pessimism, supporting hope, and programming towards pleasantry and better outcomes.

A judicial minimization of the mandatory maximum could flip the mental images dramatically for the prisoners. While the reality could later be influenced by many factors, we each live in the now of what exists at this time, and we react to the facts we see.

The reality of maximum versus minimum could flip the idea of the size of the mountain to be climbed so that a prisoner can embrace survival and plan for cooperation instead of resistance.

Mental environment is a subtle yet powerful factor in the total experience of everybody in everything. We get influenced by the people and space that we are in at any time and our own interpretation of what that means to us.

It is essential that the optimal ideas are suggested for prisoners' discernment so that they do not feel powerless and hopeless and doomed.

Optimism after sentencing can promote the best outcomes for prisoners. Pessimism after sentencing anticipates undesirable **consequences** from the situation and is not helpful.

11

6 - Judging with Limited Options

A judge who has studied Law as a career knows the situation in each case better than anyone else in the courtroom and anywhere else. How is it conscionable for our society to tie the hands of the judges when it comes to ruling on the life of a defendant when the judge believes in a fairer reality?

It is not, and we need to go back to The Declaration of our Independence and read the words - "We hold these truths to be self-evident, that all men are created equal, that they are endowed by their Creator with certain unalienable Rights, that among these are Life, Liberty and the pursuit of Happiness."

We need to set our judges free to declare sentencing with specificity in a reasonable way that, while reviewable by higher courts, is not limited to "throwing the baby out with the bathwater (anon.)."   See an example of what the judges said below from the 2010 USSC Judges' Survey.

Survey Table 15 Questions 2
{From Chapter 6 -- *Judges And An Angel Rule On Possibilities:*
We Can Cut Sentences & Prison Costs}

"The Commission should amend USSG §5K1.1 to authorize judges to sentence below the applicable guideline range to reflect a defendant's substantial assistance, even if the government does not make a motion."

Answered by 632 Abstain - 7

Two Largest Answers Total 54% Agree

7 - Red Tape

We the taxpayers need a way to cut through the red tape and take a message forward to the government that is clear and unmistakable. If only there was a simple way to do that.

8 - Voters Can Change the Rules

The power of the voting booth can change all the rules. I propose that we flip the thinking that is not working, cultivate the expansion of ideas that can improve outcomes, and program new goals.

Mass incarceration is the reality that stifles the hope of many people. We need to change the rules.

We can prevent some complications by changing the discussions and the inevitable realities. The judges are forced to deal with an antiquated system that is not working.

We can give the judges the authority to be creative and increase our options. We need to reassess all the possibilities for the kind of society that we would like to have.

A big success in prisons is the ability to spend taxpayers money and reap the relatively little benefit. The outcome for many prisoners is a cycle of pain, reactivity, and failure to thrive.

We need optimized potentials, and it will take a lot of work to make that happen. Mandatory minimum sentencing may be a significant obstacle to our success.

Mandatory minimum sentences could be replaced with compulsory rehabilitation efforts and maximum creativity and engagement. It seems like a great time to reset our priorities and reprogram for success. Let's begins the journey where and how.

9 - We Can Vote

10 - What Would We Vote For?

Writing laws is not easy, and everybody wants to have their say and government has the responsibility of dotting the "Is" and crossing the "Ts." We have the responsibility to get across what we want just like we did with the Declaration of Independence.

The Federal Government has the Senate and the House of Representatives, and they have the staff to do all the diligence that we could possibly need.

We need to convey to them what it is that we want. But do we know exactly? Probably not.

I

Think

We

Want

To

Allow

Judges

To

Cut

Mandatory

Minimum

Sentences

11 – Political Action Plan

The Bible told us all what to do. Ask for the changes that you would like to see. Seek those answers, and as you go, it shall open to you.

Ask, and it shall be given you;
seek, and ye shall find;
knock, and it shall be opened unto you:
                                                            Matthew 7:7

It is essential to be clear when asking politicians for action. I have drafted five declarations that you can copy and use for your community if you choose.

You can also write your own and please note that more people saying the same thing can increase the chances for success.

I have drafted formats for the US Congress, US Senate, State Congress, State Senate and a City format. Please edit to suit your own particular community.

Networking is Great!

Politicians in your city, village or town already have enough complainers. They are not seeking more so it would be wise to be a networker and not present yourself as one who wants to complain to your representatives.

The staff of all politicians usually delight in meeting the constituents of their leaders because it is a very efficient way for them to learn how they can serve. When you share your concerns, it helps them to prepare to serve you and your neighbors.

When many people say the same thing, they will get it. These same people that are trying to serve may also become your advocates, so networking might be something to consider.

If you take an interest in the community, people within it can take an interest in you and your affairs.

12 - Proposed Declaration to US Congress

We the people of the United States of America wish to convey to you, our esteemed representatives, that we are tremendously unhappy with the volume of our brother and sister citizens who are currently incarcerated. We feel that the laws in place are antiquated and threaten our freedom.

With all due respect, we implore you as our representatives to take on the task of fixing this problem. The social fabric of our communities needs to be protected from burdensome legal complications of the lengthy sentences created by the Mandatory Minimums.

We assert herewith the will of the people to empower the Judges to cut the sentences for non-violent offenders at the discretion of the Judges when they deem appropriate.

We would like to see the sentencing cut substantially and declare that 47% (Forty-Seven Percent) is not an unrealistic number. We would actually prefer if the average exceeded 22% (Twenty-Two Percent).

We trust Your diligence in the compliance with our wishes.

13 - Proposed Declaration to US Senate

We the people of the United States of America wish to convey to you, our esteemed representatives, that we are tremendously unhappy with the volume of our brother and sister citizens who are currently incarcerated. We feel that the laws in place are antiquated and threaten our freedom.

With all due respect, we implore you as our representatives to take on the task of fixing this problem. The social fabric of our communities needs to be protected from burdensome legal complications of the lengthy sentences created by the Mandatory Minimums.

We assert herewith the will of the people to empower the Judges to cut the sentences for non-violent offenders at the discretion of the Judges when they deem appropriate.

We would like to see the sentencing cut substantially and declare that 47% (Forty-Seven Percent) is not an unrealistic number. We would actually prefer if the average exceeded 22% (Twenty-Two Percent).

We trust Your diligence in the compliance with our wishes.

14 - Proposed Declaration to State Congress

We the people of the State of _____
wish to convey to you, our esteemed representatives,
that we are tremendously unhappy with the volume of
our brother and sister citizens who are currently
incarcerated. We feel that the laws in place are
antiquated and threaten our freedom.

With all due respect, we implore you as our
representatives to take on the task of fixing this
problem. The social fabric of our communities needs to
be protected from burdensome legal complications of
the lengthy sentences created by the Mandatory
Minimums.

**We assert herewith the will of the people to
empower the Judges to cut the sentences for non-
violent offenders at the discretion of the Judges
when they deem appropriate.**

We would like to see the sentencing cut substantially
and declare that 47% (Forty-Seven Percent) is not an
unrealistic number. We would actually prefer if the
average exceeded 22% (Twenty-Two Percent).

We trust Your diligence in the compliance with our
wishes.

15 - Proposed Declaration to State Senate

We the people of the State of _____
wish to convey to you, our esteemed representatives,
that we are tremendously unhappy with the volume of
our brother and sister citizens who are currently
incarcerated. We feel that the laws in place are
antiquated and threaten our freedom.

With all due respect, we implore you as our
representatives to take on the task of fixing this
problem. The social fabric of our communities needs to
be protected from burdensome legal complications of
the lengthy sentences created by the Mandatory
Minimums.

**We assert herewith the will of the people to
empower the Judges to cut the sentences for non-
violent offenders at the discretion of the Judges
when they deem appropriate.**

We would like to see the sentencing cut substantially
and declare that 47% (Forty-Seven Percent) is not an
unrealistic number. We would actually prefer if the
average exceeded 22% (Twenty-Two Percent).

We trust Your diligence in the compliance with our
wishes.

16 - Proposed Declaration to the City_____

We the people of _____
wish to convey to you, our esteemed representatives,
that we are tremendously unhappy with the volume of
our brother and sister citizens who are currently
incarcerated. We feel that the laws in place are
antiquated and threaten our freedom.

With all due respect, we implore you as our
representatives to take on the task of fixing this
problem. The social fabric of our communities needs to
be protected from burdensome legal complications of
the lengthy sentences created by the Mandatory
Minimums.

**We assert herewith the will of the people to
empower the Judges to cut the sentences for non-
violent offenders at the discretion of the Judges
when they deem appropriate.**

We would like to see the sentencing cut substantially
and declare that 47% (Forty-Seven Percent) is not an
unrealistic number. We would actually prefer if the
average exceeded 22% (Twenty-Two Percent).

We trust Your diligence in the compliance with our
wishes.

23

17 - Wrap Up

There can be great value in openness to others and willingness to hear their views.

These ideas will not fix the incarceration problem, but they may help stabilize and reduce the level of incarceration which can maintain lower occupancy levels and help to alleviate overcrowding which itself can improve the quality of the prison experience for many.

These ideas can also help to diminish the collateral damage to children and communities who are seriously disserved by the absoluteness of current sentencing practices.

While we need to keep the communities safe, being too rigid does not help the government to provide for all the people. Common sense can be a staunch ally to rehabilitating prisoners.

While some may argue against second chances, I think it best that those who will eventually reenter the community be ready and able to survive their release and stay free productive contributors to our society.

Avoiding recidivism through first term rehabilitation and sentence truncations can go a long way to resolving mass incarceration and bringing more quality of life to the communities of America.

Family life can be enhanced through unification as early as possible.

For
Considering
These
Ideas

Ever

It Does Not Help Prayer Still Does!

Resource: http://Create-A-Prayer.com

20 - Books Category Resources
at www.Amazon.com

Distant Healing (or Mail List) e-mail mikewann@voicenet.com

Veterans Healing Six Pack plus 2
http://angelraphaelspeaks.com/healing-books/veterans/

PTSD Power Pack
http://angelraphaelspeaks.com/healing-books/ptsd/

Angel Raphael Speaks Series & Other Angel Books
http://angelraphaelspeaks.com/

Reiki
http://angelraphaelspeaks.com/healing-books/reiki/

Children
http://angelraphaelspeaks.com/healing-books/children/

Emergency Medical Kindness
http://angelraphaelspeaks.com/healing-books/emergency-medical-kindness/

Cancer
http://angelraphaelspeaks.com/healing-books/cancer/

Addictions
http://angelraphaelspeaks.com/healing-books/addictions/

Miscellaneous Healing
http://angelraphaelspeaks.com/healing-books/misc-healing/

Prison Books - 50+ Prison Books
http://angelraphaelspeaks.com/prison-books/

21 - Angels Please Prayers

Addict's

Angels of Healing Selected
Help Me to Stay Directed
Come To Me From The Sky
I Am Ready to Succeed Not Try
If I Don't Invite You In
I Might Not Win
I Have Been Lost For Too Long
Help Me To Stay Strong

Alcoholic's

Angels of Healing On High
Help Me to Stay Dry
Come To Me From The Sky
I Am Ready to Succeed Not Try
If I Don't Invite You In
I Might Not Win
I Have Been Lost For Too Long
Help Me To Stay Strong

From

http://AngelRaphaelSpeaks.com/AAAAAAA/
The Link Above Has the Core Messages from the book on drop-down pages.

22 - Private Channeling

Angel Raphael Speaks a series of free messages that are channeled through Reverend Mike Wanner for the Highest good and Highest Healing of all concerned.

Many questions arise about Reverend Mike doing private channeling, and he does help with that so E-mail him.

Reverend Mike is available worldwide as a psychic channel, emotional release facilitator, spiritual energy practitioner & teacher, and public speaker. He looks forward to meeting you soon! Email - mikewann@voicenet.com 215-342-1270

PRIVATE SPIRITUAL READINGS/channelings or Spiritual Healing Sessions: Telephone or in person.

Rev. Mike is available for individual, intuitive one-on-one sessions with you, his Guide Family, and your Guides. He helps by offering clarity on emotional situations about your life, your purpose, your spirituality, and your release of stuffed emotions and cellular memory.

Connect to the love of your Guides today!

For more information, Please visit

http://angelraphaelspeaks.com/channel/

23 - Reverend Mike Wanner

Rev. Mike Wanner started his spiritual and ministerial studies with Reiki in 1993 and had studied seven styles of Reiki in the U.S., Japan, Canada, Denmark and Australia. He is certified to teach. He became certified to teach Integrated Energy Therapy in 1999 and co-taught the first IET class of the new Millennium. Mike began dowsing in 2001.

Ordained as an Interfaith Minister of the Circle of Miracles Ministry and a Metaphysical Minister of the International Metaphysical Ministry, Rev. Mike practices and teaches spiritual energy therapies in the Philadelphia Area.

Rev. Mike holds ministerial degrees from the University of Metaphysics and the University of Sedona. He is a Pastoral Care Associate at Jefferson - Frankford Hospital. He taught at the National Academy of Massage Therapy and Health Sciences.

Rev. Mike was a faculty member of the Medical Mission Sister's Center for Human Integration's School of Integrated Body/Mind Therapies in Fox Chase, Philadelphia, PA for twelve years.

For a complete Biography, Please visit
http://ReverendMikeWanner.com/Bio